LET'S TALK ABOUT

FEELING AFRAID

by Joy Berry • Illustrated by Maggie Smith

SCHOLASTIC INC.

New York Toronto London Auckland Sydney

ISBN 0-590-62384-2

12 11 10 9 8 7 6 5 4 3 2 1   5 6 7 8 9/9 0/0

Printed in the U.S.A.   24
First Scholastic printing, December 1995

Hello, my name is Squeaky.

I live with Kim.

Sometimes Kim feels afraid.

Sometimes he feels afraid that someone or something is going to hurt him.

I hear something outside. What if it comes in through my window and grabs me?

Sometimes Kim feels afraid that he might do something that will hurt him.

Sometimes Kim feels afraid when he doesn't know what is going to happen.

When you feel afraid, you feel scared.

Your body might do strange things when you feel afraid.

Your heart might beat faster.

You might breathe harder.

You might perspire more.

Your stomach might feel upset.

Your muscles might feel tense.

You might feel weak.

You might suddenly need to go to the bathroom.

You might feel helpless when you are afraid.

You might feel like running away.

Most of the time you won't like the things that make you feel afraid.

You might not want to be around them.

Feeling afraid isn't good if it keeps you from doing things you need to do.

Feeling afraid is good if it warns you that you are in danger.

Some people pretend they never feel afraid so others will think they are big and brave.

It's better to admit when you are afraid.

Talk to other people about your feelings.

Ask questions about the things that are scaring you.

Sometimes you'll find out that you don't need to be afraid of what is scaring you.

If you are afraid because you are in danger, try to get away from whatever is scaring you.

If you can't get away from whatever is scaring you, be careful when you are around it.

Avoid doing things that will scare you.

Avoid watching scary movies.

Avoid listening to scary stories.

Avoid thinking scary thoughts that aren't true.

Remember that everyone feels afraid.

Feeling afraid is okay.

The important thing is to do whatever you can to resolve your fear.